UNCONDITIONAL SUCCESS

DEVELOP THE ABILITY TO SUCCEED UNDER ANY CIRCUMSTANCE

DEBORA R. NELSON

Copyright © 2019 Debora R. Nelson.

All rights reserved. No part of this publication may be reproduced, distributed, or transmitted in any form or by any means, including photocopying, recording, or other electronic or mechanical methods, without the prior written permission of the publisher, except in the case of brief quotations embodied in critical reviews and certain other noncommercial uses permitted by copyright law. For permission requests, write to the publisher, addressed "Attention: Permissions Coordinator," at the address below.

www.debora.r.nelson@gmail.com – Author Debora R. Nelson

www.jesuscoffeeandprayer@gmail.com – Publishing House

Scriptures marked NIV are taken from the NEW INTERNATIONAL VERSION (NIV): Scripture taken from THE HOLY BIBLE, NEW INTERNATIONAL VERSION ®. Copyright© 1973, 1978, 1984, 2011 by Biblica, Inc.™. Used by permission of Zondervan

Scriptures marked NKJV are taken from the NEW KING JAMES VERSION (NKJV): Scripture taken from the NEW KING JAMES VERSION®. Copyright© 1982 by Thomas Nelson, Inc. Used by permission. All rights reserved

ISBN: 978-0-9998188-9-3

Publisher/Editor:

Jesus, Coffee, and Prayer Christian Publishing House

400 West Peachtree St NW STE 4-5055

Atlanta, GA 30308

www.jesuscoffeeandprayer.com

Full Cover/Format/Interior Design: Eswari Kamireddy

Author Photo: Make-up artist Randall S. Mckeehan and Photographer Sapphire Photography and Media, LLC

DEDICATION

To those who are striving to be successful. The best is yet to come. You are strong, capable, and can achieve anything that you put your mind to. You were created to experience the finer things in life, and nothing is too far out of your reach. Although you may stumble or take the occasional wrong turn on your journey towards success, be sure to take those moments as learning opportunities. You may be delayed but YOU are not denied.

The power to succeed is in your prayer, the power to succeed is in your mind, the power to succeed is within you.

Let's unleash your power.

Respectfully,

Debora R. Nelson

ENDORSEMENTS

"Unconditional Success is a great read; it confirms and brings back to mind awareness of the struggles in our successes. Stay the course and always remember Success comes with perseverance and listening to the voice of God."

Very Respectfully,
Allison E Watkins
Colonel, United States Army

"WOW!!! Is truly an understatement for this body of work. Author Debora Nelson has truly encompassed the true essence of how one can implement daily steps in pursuit of "unconditional success". A 30-week guide outlining steps to unconditional success by dissecting the many whys. She helps readers eliminate the excuses or crutches in our very own self-defeating mindsets. This is not your usual "self-help" guidance. Author Debora Nelson has given her readers both practical and biblical solutions to obtaining Unconditional Success!"

Evangelist Evonn Firms

2x Bestselling Author/CEO & Founder of The Latter Rain Project/ SKMinistries

FB@EvonnFirms

"I've known Debora from very early in her Army career and I cannot tell you how impressed I am with this book! Her willingness to share her experiences to help others find purpose & success within themselves is inspiring. She did a great job breaking down numerous practical steps to focus your journey with mental and physical actions. Great work!"

Brandon White

"Must read for Leaders, Veterans, Moms, Dads, Everybody! I am convinced that this book was written for me. While reading it, I was forced to be deal with the "Real Me." From the first chapter, the author encourages us to apply life-changing principles that have helped me re-define and re-connect with my goals and relationships. This book/guide is sure to remain in my digital library and will be revisited each year!"

Dr. Tonya Blackmon

Strategist, Author, Podcast Host (Conglomerate Empowerment CEO & Founder)

Reach me @ linktr.ee/drtonyab7

ACKNOWLEDGEMENTS

So many people have supported me on my journey. If you are not mentioned by name, it is not because I find your support less significant. I truly appreciate every spoken word of affirmation and sound advice that you gave me and will forever return the favor.

First and foremost, I would like to thank my Lord and Savior for instilling this vision and using me as a vessel to speak to his precious people. Thank you for trusting me with this responsibility as I do not take this for granted. Continue to use me in a mighty way for Your glory. *I give myself away* so that you can use me to bring about exposure to your greatness. You are true to your word and I thank you. This is only the beginning; I will continue to give any recognition, praise or honor directly back to you because without you I would be nothing. Through the good and the bad times in life you've been there, and I am forever grateful for your mercy. When the world told me that I was nothing, you've proved them wrong once again because I am your child who reigns in the very image of you here on Earth. I would be remised if I didn't thank you for this transformation. This time last year, I didn't know my true purpose here on earth, but now I know that my trial and tribulations were not for anything but to stand as a living testimony and speak on your glorious works.

To my Mother, my rock. Thank you for instilling in me the true definition of hard work and dedication. You raised Tareia and I to be strong women. You exceeded any daughter's expectations as a role model. You've always told me that "knowledge is power" and that there wasn't anything in this world that I couldn't have. You showed me how to be a true woman of God by being the same person that you are inside and outside of the church. You embedded prayer into our family and led by example by seeking God first in everything that you do. Thank you for always supporting my wildest ideas and my biggest dreams. To you, it's normal and attainable and for that, I love you. You taught me to walk in any and every room like I own it and to never hide the woman that I am. You taught me how to be unapologetically great and look good while doing it. Your soul is pure, and you are full of so much wisdom that I wish that the world could hear. Thank you for being my number one cheerleader and reminding me that "no weapon formed against me shall prosper," and it hasn't

To my Father, how near and dear you are to my heart—I will forever be a daddy's girl. Thank you for being present, sowing guidance and strength into my life. You've taught me how to take the good with the bad and how to survive in any circumstances. Thank you for not shielding me from life by reminding me that there will be some days of disappointment and other days with grief but to trust God through it all. Your words have never failed me even during my weakest moments. Thank you for always putting a smile on my face and reminding me that *I am not just a Soldier in the Army but a Soldier in the army of the Lord*. I will forever be prepared for war and will fight every battle with my strongest weapon— *the word of God. I could not have chosen a better Father. I love you with all that is in me.*

To my Sister Tareia, I look up to you and admire your growth and beauty. Thank you for leading by example; you are a great mother and a woman with a selfless heart. You put everyone before you; (including me and your children- you are a wonderful mother) and I thank you. You would literally give me the shirt off your back and I would never take that for granted. Thank you for always reminding me who I am and what to never accept in this lifetime. Thank you for reinforcing my worth and never backing down on my behalf. I could not have chosen a better sibling to go through life with. Do you remember the many times that I said that I would write a book? Well, here it is. Because of people like you in my life, I believed that it was possible. Because of you, I will never give up. Even if I get tired or worn out, I will pick myself up, start over again, and keep moving forward, just like you.

You can create a masterpiece out of dust, and I will continue to emulate you.

To Gabrielle, thank you for being a friend and sister of your word. You never changed and I am thankful to have a transparent, honest, and loyal friend in my corner. You unselfishly feed our friendship and I am forever grateful. You are a great wife and mother (I labeled you *wife* before your wedding; I see it in your future.) I pray to be half as good as you when it's my turn. While we may have been distant for the greatest part of our friendship, you've always remained consistent and true. I can't thank you enough. You are my Sister.

To Ashley, I am thankful for your listening ear, love, and sisterhood. You are amazing and I am excited to see what God has in store for you.

You are full of talent, beauty, and intelligence. I am thankful that God added you to my Sister circle. While we are completely different, we too have so much in common. Thank you for being supportive through my trials and tribulations. Thank you for never judging me during my weakest moments. Most of all, thank you for being you.

To Brittani, I cannot thank God enough for placing you in my life—A true Sister indeed. Our friendship is weathered and has been exercised from many countries apart for many years now. Thank you for showing me the true definition of sisterhood. You have a big heart, a bright soul, and a lasting impression like no other. Thank you for believing in me. I couldn't have done this without your words of encouragement and love.

To Eric, thank you for support and guidance. I am so ever grateful that I have you in my corner. You speak life and add value to my life. Thank you for opening my eyes to see life from a different perspective. You taught me the true importance of relationships. You've seen me at my worst, and you've seen me at my best, but your love and support remain constant. You are the hardest working man that I know with the ability to perform under and through any circumstance. You are the true definition of "Unconditional Success."

To First Sergeant Bryan Corbet Sr., thank you for your loyalty and friendship. You are a leader who is true to his word and I pray nothing but success and happiness for you and your beautiful family. Never change who you are or how you lead. Not just the Army but the world needs more people like you. You're authentic in what you do, and you can impact lives. Continue to wear the body of armor; continue to do God's work. He's not done with you yet, there's more in store and He will forever be with you.

For those of you that are currently serving in the military.

You are the ignored community. You are the community that requires the most motivation. You give your all and when you encounter challenges, you are expected to remain mentally, physically, and spiritually strong. But trust me, I understand. I understand that whether you are a woman or a man, we all have limits. Once those limits are tried, you have to dig deep to stay motivated and to not give up. If you're reading this, it is not by coincidence; this devotional is for you. For those of you who are trying to figure out why you may be in a certain situation that may not seem favorable for your career progression, your health, or maybe even your family, this devotional is for you.

Lastly, to my nana- Loretta Nelson and Aunt Donna who both passed away to cancer in 2019, I am forever grateful for the love that you both showed me and thankful for the time we spent. You both will forever be in my heart. I will continue to build upon our family's legacy. I will not let either of you down. I never officially grieved because of God's peace. I know that you both are looking down and protecting our family. Rest in heaven beautiful ladies. I love you both.

This book was started less than a year ago. I saw the vision that God instilled in me and I trusted it.

CONTENTS

DEDICATION III
ENDORSEMENTS V
ACKNOWLEDGEMENTS VII
FOREWORD XV
WEEK 1 Isolating yourself for Greatness and How to Endure It: Alone and Unafraid 1
WEEK 2 Building Friendships that Feed You and not Deplete You- Preserving your Energy for your Journey to Success 5
WEEK 3 Understanding the Power of Peace- Incorporating Peace into your Daily Routine 9
WEEK 4 Learning when to take and let go of control- Trusting your Process 13
WEEK 5 Setting your pride aside 15
WEEK 6 Developing a Path to Success that will Benefit Others Around you- Building a Kingdom rather than just a Temple .. 19
WEEK 7 Learning How to Wait while Enjoying the Process 23
WEEK 8 Developing an Active Support Team 25
WEEK 9 Appreciating the People and Time Spent along the Way- Taking nothing for Granted 27
WEEK 10 How to Renew your Strength during Moments of Weakness 31
WEEK 11 Validating your Growth-Isolate, Reflect, and put in Action 33
WEEK 12 How Judging a Book by its Cover can keep you From Connecting to Greatness! 37
WEEK 13 Embracing Change and Making it Work for You 41
WEEK 14 Speaking Power into your Mind 43

WEEK 15 Turning Failure into Motivation 45
WEEK 16 Walking in Your Blessings 49
WEEK 17 Trusting God's Plan for You 51
WEEK 18 Cherishing Ordained Connections
with Others 55
WEEK 19 Understanding your Purpose 59
WEEK 20 Learning to Push Pass Fear 61
WEEK 21 Developing a Winner's Mindset 63
WEEK 22 Properly Measuring your Strength 67
WEEK 23 Learning to Identify Distractors
through Reflection 71
WEEK 24 Taking "No" for an Answer 73
WEEK 25 Performing when Challenged 77
WEEK 26 Shaping your True Identity 79
WEEK 27 Fighting a War while Tired 83
WEEK 28 Succeeding with Failure 87
WEEK 29 Growing in an Unknown Environment. 89
WEEK 30 Using Knowledge as Your Power 91

FOREWORD

"I can do all things through Christ who strengthens me."
Philippians 4:13

This book is a direct reflection of how I used Philippians 4:13 to get through a breaking point in my career. I was inspired to write this book to sow hope into the lives of others. After encountering a breaking point, I was unsure of my purpose and even questioned who I was, all because I allowed other people to speak over my life instead of listening to what God spoke over my life. My life became a living testimony when I began to live and operate by Philippians 4:13. I started to speak and act on words of affirmation. I stepped out of my comfort zone and began operating in discomfort to accomplish goals while believing, "I can do all things through Christ who strengthens me". If you truly believe that there is nothing in this world that you cannot accomplish with the Lord by your side, you will not fail. You cannot fail. I know that you have moments where you feel uncertain about your life and question your purpose. You are not alone, just hang on tight and trust that everything will work out for your good. You don't have to figure out life in just one day. You have an entire life to live, experience, and enjoy. Yes, I said enjoy! You don't need to have all the answers at this time or see the entire vision for it to come into fruition, but if you believe that you can fulfill your purpose, you will accomplish more than you could ever imagine. I was inspired to write this devotional to empower and encourage every one of you to not give up on accomplishing your goals, even the goals that you may have pushed to the side for years. It doesn't matter who you are or what status you've obtained in life, we all have a bit of insecurity about where we believe we should be in life and where we are.

We don't want to admit it but the true reason why we have not accomplished the goals that we once envisioned is that we've either lost hope or confidence in ourselves or we've allowed external factors to delay our progression. But what you must realize is that you are in total control of your mindset and your ability to win.

This devotional is to remind you that you can overturn those mental roadblocks; you are capable of developing a plan that will put you in the position to conquer those setbacks. The longer we allow distractions or challenging moments to stop us from moving forward, the less we touch and impact lives. We lose the ability to break generational curses; negative behavior or habits that impact a bloodline for generations. For some of you reading this book, the goals that you are trying to accomplish are in pursuit of changing your family's legacy and your family's legacy is depending on your ability to succeed! You have to get this right. You were put on this Earth for a reason and you are the only one who can carry out your assigned mission because you are fearfully and wonderfully made.

In thirty weeks, you will be in the position to accomplish the goals that you've set out. You will be more courageous, and I pray that you will be more action forward on the road towards success. You are about to enter into a dimension that will push you out of your comfort zone directly into your purpose which will enable you to exceed daily expectations from people around you. This devotional is a step-by-step 30-week empowering guide that will condition your mind and soul to identify, tackle, and overcome the areas in your life that are preventing you from reaching the next level of greatness. This devotional was written for those who are on a mission to reveal and strengthen areas of weaknesses to dominate and elevate in life— is that you?

This devotional comes with a bonus feature— the next 30 weeks will train you to successfully obtain unconditional success.

What is unconditional success you might ask? Unconditional success is the ability to obtain success that is not determined by external factors i.e.., networking, evaluations, etc. Unconditional success is earned through internal factors such as prayer, individual plans, strength, and consistency. Unconditional success cannot be delayed by outside factors because it's not dependent on external factors (people, social class, finances); it is solely dependent on what's inside of you. Just like Jesus loves us unconditionally, we are not loved by the Lord when we are doing everything right. We are loved by the Lord no matter who we are and what we have done. But it is still our responsibility to work to sustain the unconditional love by staying in the word and building and maintaining a relationship with the Lord which is a precedence to unconditional success. Success is available to us all but we must work hard to secure and elevate our success. Wouldn't it be amazing if you were able to master the ability to consistently work towards and accomplish your goals no matter the conditions of an environment to include your supervisor or unforeseen issues like divorce or depression?

Would you believe me if I told you that this devotional was written to transform you into an individual of consistency and everlasting success?

Everlasting success is achievable, but it requires the correct mindset. Reaching your maximum potential with this devotional will be easier than you could imagine. No matter the career field or your position, there will always be challenges and those challenges will happen often. *Ask yourself, how can you develop yourself into a person who can exceed expectations without breaking and falling completely off track every single time you encounter a challenge or road block?*

There was a reason that you purchased this book, there was something that you were lacking, and you saw this as an opportunity to feed your mind and soul. You expected a life changing experience which makes this the first step in the right direction toward acquiring the ability to consistently forward progress. I can guarantee you that this purchase was not by mistake or chance. This book was purposed for you for where you currently are in your life or even the pursuit of your career. Maybe you're not where you want to be because you allowed yourself to get pulled by the current of a relationship, organization, or by your circumstances rather than the vision that God has imparted in your mind and heart. Maybe you would be much further along if you didn't allow your emotions or mind traps to determine your success or lack thereof. *There is a method to the madness, or shall we say there is a method to unconditional success?*

I can almost bet you that you decided to invest in this book because you read the title and just knew that the information in this book is exactly what you were looking for— better yet, what you needed to push yourself to your fullest potential. Well, guess what? You're right. I wrote this book with you in mind! This book was written for YOU! I wrote this book for the person who needed a bit more inspiration (Is that you?), the person who had doubts (Is this you too?), the person who redirected their path but somehow became slightly off track because of temporary situations in life or in and out of the workplace that dominated the ability to maintain stability and focus (I'm pretty sure this is you too).

The good news is, you are not alone. You are never alone. When writing this book, I thought less of what I wanted to say and more of what God wanted me to say on his behalf. But even better, I've been you, I am you and I draw lessons off my personal experiences and ability to overcome to directly relate to some of the challenges that you might be going through. I was dedicated to ensuring that God's message was delivered to YOU no matter the time, dedication, and discipline it took to deliver his word. With being a messenger comes with a price and let's just say that the price is quite high because no one wants to take advice from a person who hasn't lived it. I've endured and I am living proof of God's glory. He is real and His word and power never goes void. His truth will forever stand and those who trust in the Lord will forever be rewarded, protected, and guided through the dark or danger. I am here to tell you that those prayers you've been praying and those visions you've been having can happen; but require stabilization to sustain it.

Let explain- Stabilization is the key to victory. An unstable person's capability to focus with a positive forward-thinking mindset is limited under this condition. Instability can cloud one's judgement or block visions. More importantly, instability can limit a person's ability to see long term wins. Living an unstable life can be very difficult and can be compared to a premature seed. Some people never get the opportunity to see the tree (blessing/accomplished goals) that blossoms from the planted seed (vision) because they've allowed storm after storm to sweep through their town (mind) and pull the roots out over and over again. Can you imagine having a vision, putting action towards it, and watching yourself fail over and over again because you allowed life's challenges to knock you off your feet every time? You have to learn to stand in the storm. You have to plant your feet on solid ground and develop your mind and body to withstand anything that comes your way.

Fortunately, no one is perfect, and everyone has the opportunity to develop themselves into an unmovable force. Let me take you back to a moment in time when I too doubted my abilities to become a *stabilizer* within my work environment and found it hard to truly understand what God wanted me to gain out of this particular experience.

I started writing this piece when I was deployed. I promised God that I would start a devotional for "the deployed Soldier".

That was the vision I HAD but as you see, this is the vision that God had. I just knew that I was destined to write a piece of literature that would save and protect the Soldiers who put their lives on the line to save and protect others. I soon realized through prayer that God did not intend for this book to be limited to the military. Although, those who serve are very much deserving of the honor, praise, and recognition for their selfless service, it became clear to me that there were people from different walks of life that suffer from the lack of guidance, understanding, and effectiveness within their career field. Through my travels and frequent conversations with CEOs, entrepreneurs, Senior military leaders, Senior religious leaders, 9-5 shift workers, and part-time workers, I've learned that they all had one thing in common. They all had a moment in their career where they struggled with maintaining consistency with accomplishing goals. They struggled to effectively move forward in life and in their careers because they failed to master the skill of stabilization. Realize that God has never been focused on the smaller picture. He has always created every thought with the purpose and intention of positively impacting everyone. This book is no different because I understand, know, and have spoken to people with different backgrounds and levels of experience in the workforce who struggled with elevation and forward progression.

Take a moment to reflect on yourself or those around you who struggled with elevating their circumstance and did not see a way out. Over the past year or so, I've noticed that it didn't matter the profession or age but there were doctors, lawyers, waitresses, policemen/women, fast food workers, gas attendants, and celebrities that were all dealing with challenges in their career field. It didn't matter how much income one made- they all suffered behind closed doors the same. At some point, instability from outside factors led them to believe that they were being setback without a way out and in some instances, it resulted in people either expressing suicidal ideation, attempt, or accomplishment.

Once damage was done and the story unraveled, it was revealed that those who caused physical harm to themselves were the result of lingering challenges in the workplace. People often felt worthless or embarrassed by their perceived failure. At that moment, their only way out was by taking their own life. Most of these people were ignored. Most of these people just needed a bit of hope or guidance but felt alone.

What validates my thoughts?

I'm glad you asked.

I've been that person.

I've been pushed by overwhelming challenges in my workplace- to a mental space that made me fell stuck.

No matter what I did, said, or attempted to do, I was not valued, recognized, or good enough due to a temporary toxic work environment.

Did you catch that?

TEMPORARY toxic work environment.

For the majority of my career, I received nothing but praise, recognition, and glory. In those environments I excelled, I was the best version of myself. But it became very challenging and almost impossible to dig myself out of a hole within an environment that did not set perimeters to succeed.

Due to this situation, I not only lost hope on the job, I also lost hope in my personal life.

I stopped working on goals.

I didn't have a vision.

I questioned my career.

It was by the grace of God that He opened my eyes! In order to become the woman that God pre-destined for me to be, I had to discover a stabilized mindset to succeed!

Stabilization was the important factor to help propel my performance and sharpen the leadership skills required to lead a team who counted on me!

Once I realized the true power of stability, I also learned that I was in control of acquiring and sustaining unconditional success. Once I developed this mindset, became in control of my happiness, and my success, *I became an unstoppable force in and out of the workplace.*

In result of this mindset I no longer worry about the pressures of an evaluation because I know my worth and what I bring to the table. If I was to lose my current career today or tomorrow, I would be successful because I put 110% percent into professionally and personally developing myself. This mindset breaks chains.

I no longer walk on egg shells at work because those who chose to value me-will and those who don't can't stop my ability to succeed.

Why?

Because those who are postured to succeed will succeed in any environment or under any conditions. Success does not mean that you won't fail. It means that you won't lose your focus and you won't give up when times are rough. Success means that you chose to wake up every morning, get dress, and conquer the day. Success means that you know your purpose even when the stars don't align, even when you don't have anyone cheering you on. Success is also being a living example, staying motivated and pushing forward to influence a thriving culture around you. Your thought process can and will impact those around you so it's critical that you are pushing out consistency and positivity.

There was a moment in time or even currently where you doubted your skill, level of competence, or ability to succeed. I am here to reassure you that you have what it takes to reach your maximum potential no matter the conditions that are set. You are a trailblazer and you too can obtain unconditional success!

WEEK 1
ISOLATING YOURSELF FOR GREATNESS AND HOW TO ENDURE IT: ALONE AND UNAFRAID

Proverbs 8:30 "Then I was by him, as one brought up with him; and I was daily his delight, rejoicing always before him."

NOTES FROM THE AUTHOR

To isolate yourself for greatness, you have to learn how to be alone and unafraid. There will be times where you may not quite understand the plan that God has for you but trust that his plan is greater than your imagination. There is power in knowing that you are purposed with strength and courage to endure even in the darkest nights. Although you will be connected with many people along your journey, it is important to understand that your journey will require you to travel alone; but have comfort in knowing that God is with you every step of the way! In whatever you do, serve without fear. Position yourself to focus without a doubt. Trust in the skills and gifts that the Lord has imparted in you- for you were uniquely designed to fulfill the purpose that lies inside of you.

Truly, there is a reason for every season.

As a Soldier in the United States Army, deployments have a funny way of making me feel like I was uprooted from my lifestyle and abruptly placed out of my comfort zone. Deployments have torn me away and caused an emotional eruption every time I had to move out of a home where I've created memories and friends. Although temporary, it felt like the longest periods of isolation in my life. Learning from my previous experiences, I've grown to understand that deployments allow a period to *reset and refocus.*

I've realized that he anxiety of being temporary separated from family and friends was a slight hurdle that I needed to cross in order to focus on what was required of me. I had to shift my mind the moment I planted my feet on the flight and before boarding the plane to depart. Between the bottom step of the aircraft and my assigned seat I knew that I was going through the transition phase of my deployment. I was departing from the known and entering into the unknown: different location, culture, and work environment. I didn't have a choice to board the plane, but I did have the *choice* to change my mindset. My new mindset accepted and embraced isolation.

Reflecting on my deployments, I've gained new friends and lost relationships which served for the greater good of my life. Those temporary pauses revealed those who would stick by my side and those who wouldn't. This ultimately impacted my ability to shape a solid and consistent support team.

I remember when I received my ninety-day notification to deploy to Poland. *Instead of emotionally fighting against it, I decided to set a goal.*

For that particular deployment, I decided to focus on ways to turn this period of isolation into an opportunity for growth and restoration.

I made a cognitive decision to start writing this very devotional. I trained my mind to focus more on what I could gain from this particular experience and how I could share those experiences with others in hopes of making someone else's life easier. I also decided to *focus* my attention towards the excitement of returning home rather than what I left behind. Forward-thinking encourages positive thoughts of the future. During this period of isolation, *prayer was essential.* It provided me peace, guidance, and calmness. I learned the true meaning of letting go and letting God.

When I decided to be alone and unafraid, I let go and God moved on my behalf.

He placed the right people in my corner. People that helped me endure rough times. These very people were directly tied to my future work for God.

Not allowing God to take full control can limit or block the blessing(s) that the Lord has in store for you. I encourage you on this day, to let go and let God lead you in your season of isolation. Allow the Lord to open your eyes and speak to you. *Experiences in life develop and prepare us for the next level.* Allow yourself to view this moment in your life as an opportunity, rather than a hindrance and watch how you set the tone for your journey.

Call to Action

Take this week to focus on isolating for purpose. During this time, turn off your phone, social media, and embrace your environment.

Jot down a few ideas that come to mind during this period of isolation.

- What creative thoughts come to mind?
- What plans did you put in place to accomplish your goals?
- What have you had time to think about, plan, or prepare for this week that you haven't had time for because of distractions?
- Take this time to focus on areas in your life that need action and not just words~ jot it on the next page and watch your life start to *SHIFT* in a forward direction.

WEEK 2
BUILDING FRIENDSHIPS THAT FEED YOU AND NOT DEPLETE YOU~ PRESERVING YOUR ENERGY FOR YOUR JOURNEY TO SUCCESS

Proverbs 13:20 "Walk with the wise and become wise, for a companion of fools suffers harm."

Relationships should be tested. The strength of a bond should be proven. The quality of the people in which you allow in your space should be of good quality rather than quantity. Your circle can make or break you; whether it be family members, friendships, or relationships. All 'ships' must be tested.

NOTES FROM THE AUTHOR

Did you ever wake up one day and realize that your circle of "supporters" or those you believed to be supporters decreased in number? Have you ever had a moment when you realized that some of the people that you use to call for advice happen to be the same people you refuse to reach out to in a moment of triumph? Believe it or not, it's normal, healthy, and needed. The harsh reality of life is that sometimes we don't make the best decisions in determining who we should allow in our life. We don't necessarily know what we need until we need it.

Unforeseen situations have a funny way *(I use that term loosely) of* revealing how well we've done with assessing and selecting our inner circle. If you are currently in a position where you feel like your support team is small in number or non-existent, I want you to understand that you are not alone. Lacking a support team or quality support team typically exists during your transition. Temporary.

At times, it may feel that your life has fallen apart due to a lack of support. Even in those moments, take solace in knowing that one day, you will appreciate those who do support you.

After-all support is a two-way street.

Trust me, you will make it and you are not alone.

Don't come down hard on yourself if you failed to choose the right individuals to be in your support group.

Take time to assess and identify the factors that led to poor decision making and **change it**!

We are creatures of habit.

As easy as some of us may have developed the habit of allowing the wrong type of people in our lives, it's just as simple to make selecting the right type of people easy.

Call to Action

For the next week, take time to assess the persons you associate yourself with on a day to day basis and ask the hard questions.

- How does this person feed my mind, body, and soul?
- Has this person weathered a storm with me and still stuck around?
- Does this person invest in me or deplete me?
- Have I grown since this person has come into my life?
- After asking these three hard questions about family members, friendships, and/or your significant other, you should be able to determine if that is the person/person(s) that you should allow to stay in your life.

During this deployment, be strong in cutting off loose ends and be selfish for once to make decisions that will set you up for elevation and forward-thinking.

Do you know how hard it is for someone to run a race with baggage? It is impossible to run a race with too much baggage.

Eventually you will lose.

If you are currently feeling like you are losing, let's start this deployment with a win! Free yourself and let's get energized.

WEEK 3
UNDERSTANDING THE POWER OF PEACE- INCORPORATING PEACE INTO YOUR DAILY ROUTINE

John 14:27 "Peace I leave with you, my peace I give to you; not as the world gives do I give to you. Let not your heart be troubled, neither let it be afraid."

Peace— A guaranteed way to get through life's challenges on a day to day basis, free of charge. Incorporating peace into your daily routine is a firm way of telling your worries and insecurities that you mean business. Peace is a shield that provides your mind protection; allows optimal focus and the ability to think on a new level. Understanding the power of peace can prepare you to better handle disappointments or uncertainties, while also strengthening your mind, body, and soul. Allow yourself to get lost in your peaceful thoughts.

I can guarantee you that having peace of mind will give you hope and a sense of ease in knowing that everything will be just fine, no matter the situation.

NOTES FROM THE AUTHOR

Can you imagine having a world of your own where there are no worries, concerns, or doubts capable of knocking you down and where insecurities cannot faze you? What if I told you that place does exist? Believe it or not, heaven on Earth exist! You have ultimate control over the level of peace in your life. One of the glories of peace is that it's free! Have you ever taken the time to listen to interviews where multibillionaires express that even after seeing all the riches in the world, nothing fulfills or completes them like having a peace of mind?

If money solved every issue in the world, then why do some of the richest people in the world decide to end their own lives?

Think of peace like armor.

Armor protects the body part in which it covers. With peace, nothing can touch you, and it is very hard to knock you down. Having peace of mind allows you to think clearly, make sound decisions, and enjoy life for what it is. Having peace allows for better rest, a good mentally, emotionally, and healthier lifestyle.

Peace is a blessing that is afforded to everyone, not just some.

Peace is available and plentiful. Take time to clear your mind. Make a list of the factors that are currently limiting your peace. Once you identify those factors, take some time to establish solutions or just take time for acceptance.

Obtaining peace is much easier when you accept life for what it is and still chose to move forward.

Call to Action

For the next week, take the time to develop your peace strategy. Everyone needs a peace strategy!

- Your peace strategy should consist of your plan to remove anything from your life that disrupts peace and your long-term plan to maintain it.

- Jot down a few reminders to yourself that you can read in a time of uncertainty or defeat. For example, one of my little reminders would consist of, "Debora, do not forget the last time you experienced uncertainty and remember how God brought you out, he'll do it again". Or, "Debora, you were built for this, don't give up, it will all work out for your good".

WEEK 4
LEARNING WHEN TO TAKE AND LET GO OF CONTROL- TRUSTING YOUR PROCESS

1 Peter 5:7 "Cast all your anxiety on him because he cares for you."

Letting go of the things that are out of your control gives you total control.

NOTES FROM THE AUTHOR

As much as we believe that we can, it is nearly impossible to control every aspect of our lives and we would go entirely insane trying to do so. We cannot control the outside factors that tend to shake up our lives at unexpected times, but we do control how we respond to it.

We are not in control of the day nor the hour in which we wake up or go to sleep. We are not in control of the natural disasters that occur from day to day, month to month, or annually. We are not in control of when life cometh and when it leaves us. As human beings, we have the sole responsibility to control our reactions to those unexpected events because it affects those around us. We are in full control of how we speak to others when we do not get our way, or if we are still happy even when we realize that we are unable to get something that we may have desired.

It is important to accept what life throws to you and move with the punches.

Call to Action

For this week, let's focus on developing a way to be able to push forward with your dreams and aspirations while expecting the impossible to happen!

- How would you react?
- What would you do to get you through this moment?
- Who is your support channel?
- Will you keep yourself spiritually, mentally, and emotionally sound?
- What if you lost your job, what would you do?
- If you lose a family member, what is your plan to tie loose ends?

If you experience relationship heartbreak suddenly due to a cheating significant other, how would you ensure that you stayed on track with your life instead of a short or long-term pause that may potentially result in failed accomplishments or setbacks? Use this week to prepare for the unexpected!

WEEK 5
SETTING YOUR PRIDE ASIDE

Your answer will always be no if you don't ask.

NOTES FROM THE AUTHOR

There were situations in my life where I wished that I had the extra courage to speak up. I wished that I didn't allow situations to take its natural course and I also wished that I wasn't afraid to look at potential disappointment or failure in the face. I use the term "potential" lightly because fear caused me to assume that the unanswered questions that I had were going to result in disappointments or failures.

But what I eventually realized is that there were situations that did not work in my favor as a result of my failing to speak up. I also realized that some of those situations could have been prevented if I was either bold enough to address the situation or humble enough to *put pride aside*. Addressing an issue takes courage and makes you vulnerable. It is human nature to allow situations to "just happen" because many of us allow our pride to stop us from confronting issues head-on. I don't know too many people who are willing to position themselves as the target to a flying dart— the target being our pride and the flying dart being the unanswered question.

I've learned that people who address situations head-on, get the results that they want even when it seems like there isn't a solution to a problem. There is always an exception to policies that are not identified unless someone is bold enough to ask questions.

I remember when I sought guidance for my next duty assignment while attending the Army's Signal Captain's Career Course at Fort Gordon, GA.

For Captains at the career course, obtaining the right duty assignment is a critical career progression. I explained to one of the instructors that I planned on submitting a letter of introduction, my last 3 officer evaluation reports, and my officer review board documents via email to the brigade commander of the unit I wanted to take command.

It was recommended to me that I should not contact the brigade commander and that I should call the branch and if anything, send an email to his deputy brigade commander.

(Army hierarchy talk for those who may not be familiar)

Before that situation, I was dead set on submitting my email with the mentioned documents. I was excited that I managed to gain enough confidence in my professional records and faith in God. I was making the right decision to reach out to the brigade commander. I wanted to address the situation head-on and wanted my potential boss to know that I wanted to take command.

As a junior captain, it is considered unorthodox to email the brigade commander directly. I saved the email and sat on it for 72 hours. I went back and forth about it and decided that I was going to go through with it. I prayed, I reviewed my email and pressed send. I felt confident about being proactive in seeking my next duty assignment. Within 24 hours, I received an email back from my brigade commander. *The result of that email led me to write this book as a company commander for that particular unit.* Thank God I wasn't afraid of failure.

Thank God I was bolder than my doubts.

Thank God I didn't listen to the advice I was given.

Thank God I kept my faith and lastly, thank God I hit "send".

If I would have never asked the question, I would have never been selected for company commander as an officer who served a little over 5 ½ years when interviewed.

- How many questions did you leave unanswered?
- How many of those questions affected your growth or ability to succeed at a quicker rate?
- Take this week to focus on areas in your life that may be in limbo because you were afraid to ask questions.
- Jot those questions or areas down and develop a plan that will build up your confidence and humble you enough to go for it!

WEEK 6
DEVELOPING A PATH TO SUCCESS THAT WILL BENEFIT OTHERS AROUND YOU- BUILDING A KINGDOM RATHER THAN JUST A TEMPLE

Philippians 2: 3-4 "Do nothing from rivalry or conceit but in humility count others more significant than yourselves. Let each of you look not only to his interest but also to the interest of others."

In everything that you do, do it with the thought of its impact on others around you.

NOTES FROM THE AUTHOR

Do you realize that the decisions you make have a second and third order of effect? Your decisions usually impact someone or something much greater than yourself. It is important to remember that the timeliness and effectiveness of decisions that we make daily will eventually impact someone or something other than yourself.

The decisions that parents make affect their children.

The decisions that leaders make affect their subordinates.

The decisions of a Pastor affect his/her sheep. The decisions that an NFL coach ultimately makes will impact the team's ability to make it to the Super bowl.

Those who make careful decisions have the mindset of a builder. Take time to think before speaking and plan before doing. Those who make careful and well thought out decisions tend to experience more fulfillment in life than the average person. The goal is to make decisions that allow others to benefit from your thought process.

The goal is to better than those around you and the environment in which you operate. Your decisions can result in creating a promising future while increasing the quality of life around you. Would you like to be known as a builder? A person who can build within and build others around you? Pretty spectacular right?

Call to Action

Take this week to think about your impact on those around you.

Are you a builder or do you need to revamp your decision-making process?

Are you creating a world of success for others around you?

What do you bring to the table that draws people towards you?

- Write down a list of people in which you've impacted this year by making sound decisions.
- Keep this list handy whenever you need a small reminder of the impact that you're making in the world.

- Jot down a plan that will encourage you to remain consistent with considering others when making decisions.

WEEK 7
LEARNING HOW TO WAIT WHILE ENJOYING THE PROCESS

James 1:4 "And let endurance have its perfect result, so that you may be perfect and complete, lacking in nothing."

Good things come to those that wait and great things come to those who appreciate the process.

NOTES FROM THE AUTHOR

I remember when I was a child; I was so delighted to smell fresh cake baking in the oven. I couldn't wait for it to finish cooking. I desired a moist, warm, and sweet cake so that my mother and sister would think that I was the best baker in the world. I would pace back and forth across the kitchen floor, watching the clock tick. After a while, my impatience started to kick in. I used to think to myself, "This cake has to been done, it smells so good but the recipe states that it requires at least 15 additional minutes".

I began to question the recipe. I began to question the reasoning behind the cake needing to cook an additional 15 minutes if it looked cooked and smelled great. I remember pulling the cake out of the oven earlier than the recommended time due to the lack of patience. I put the icing on top and cut a slice out to taste test it before everyone else. When I slid the knife through the cake, I quickly noticed that the entire blade was covered with batter—the cake wasn't cooked.

I then realized that although something may look complete, it may require a bit more time to get the best results. I learned the importance of a process and even more so, the importance of patience. Just like cake baking in the oven, we are going through a process. We are being prepared inside and out. If the process is interrupted, it may cause us to be incomplete or unprepared for what's store for us.

Just like cake, once complete inside and out people around you will enjoy and recognize the complete and best version of you. *Don't rush the process, embrace the process.* The best version of you is still cooking in the oven; let greatness take its course.

- What is that one area of your life that seems to be taking forever to finish?
- What goal have you been working on that's been taking over a year to complete?
- Jot down that "thing" that you've been waiting for.
- List areas in your life that could use improvement and redirect your focus for the better.

WEEK 8
DEVELOPING AN ACTIVE SUPPORT TEAM

Galatians 6:2 "Carry each other's burdens, and in this way, you will fulfill the law of Christ."

It is just as important to support others as you expect others to support you.

NOTES FROM THE AUTHOR

Your support channel is built by the people that have supported you over the years. But have you ever taken a moment to think of how many of those supporters you failed to support in return? If you feel concerned about the size of your support system or feel that you lack support, it could be the result of failing to invest in others. An active support system is a two-way street. It is made of trust and dependency.

Those who support you know that you are a person of truth and in return, they extend themselves to show you their appreciation; it is your job to hold your end of the bargain. The amount of support that you extend will determine the amount that you will reap. If you take the time to extend support to others naturally, you will never lack support with the two-way support method in place because those people will feel an obligation to make sure that you never lack in that area.

Active support lends a listening ear and sound judgment. The people who chose to support you have to care about you to some degree because we know that time is more valuable than money. Those you lend your time to will extend themselves because they know that they matter to you. People view support like children view the presence of their parents. There isn't enough money to compensate for a child's missed time with their parents like there isn't enough money to compensate for a lack of support from someone you cherish.

Call to Action

- Take time this week to show your loved ones that you care and support them through action.
- Pick up the phone, send an email, or even a heart filled letter to those that you may not have shown interest in their endeavors, goals, or precious moments.
- Make a list and contact them this week! Do your part to establish your active support team. A support team is ineffective unless it's active.

WEEK 9
APPRECIATING THE PEOPLE AND TIME SPENT ALONG THE WAY- TAKING NOTHING FOR GRANTED

1 Peter 4:7 "Everything in the world is about to be wrapped up, so take nothing for granted. Stay wide-awake in prayer."

You never know what tomorrow will bring so cherish the time and the people that you have today.

NOTES FROM THE AUTHOR

Another great benefit that I've gained from being a deployed Soldier- taking advantage of today. "Live in the moment" sounds so cliché but if you pay attention to what the older generation usually wishes for, they would have "lived their life" when they were younger. Taking advantage of the present has the same concept. Spend less time worrying about what tomorrow will bring, what next week will lack, or the challenges of next year. Instead, do your best to focus on the people in your immediate area. Try to figure out how you can impact someone else's life for the better or potential lessons learned from current situations to increase the quality of life for you and others around you. Spend more time focusing on maximizing opportunities and developing a game plan. Use that game plan to capitalize on each precious opportunity.

Set aside time to pray, think, and visualize the reasoning for this very moment in life. Crossing paths with people does not happen by mistake. It's an opportunity to sow into the lives of others rather than to reap. I remember a time in my military career where I attended psychological warfare selections where I had an opportunity to meet a variety of people from across the army. There was one particular Soldier who stood out to me. This Soldier and I shared many conversations during training. At the time I was a Captain and he was a knowledgeable specialist. Little does he know that during our many conversations, I learned so much from him. I started to truly understand the hearts and minds of Soldiers through the junior enlisted lens. I remember expressing to him that I didn't plan on staying in much longer and that I wanted to complete my term and pursue my civilian goals. I explained that I was still motivated, but I felt that it was purposed for me to move forward with "my plan."

He expressed that based on his conversation with me that he believed that I was the type of leader that Soldiers needed and that he could tell that I generally cared about the troops. He could tell that I was there for a purpose rather than a title. I kind of chuckled to myself because I knew for sure that I was going to get out in about in another year or so.

Here I am today, deployed as a company commander with the primary focus to strengthen my unit's morale, legacy, and leave them in greater hands upon my departure. Through the challenges, I still manage to smile, knowing the responsibility that God has blessed me with. His very words stick with me often. To think that a Captain in the United

States Army was inspired and motivated about his words that still linger in my soul, I would like to say thank you. You know who you are; we sat in the cafeteria at Fort Bragg's special operations facility.

I am proud that you were bold enough to take that step to start your own business that is geared towards the health and welfare of our Soldiers, and the people in your community. It amazes me how bold you were to leave the known to the unknown for the betterment of others.

Call to Action

- This week take some time to make a list of people or opportunities that you may have taken for granted.

- Realign yourself and develop a plan that will lead you towards making every day, person, and opportunity count. Take nothing for granted.

WEEK 10
HOW TO RENEW YOUR STRENGTH DURING MOMENTS OF WEAKNESS

Isaiah 40:31 "But those who hope in the LORD will renew their strength. They will soar on wings like eagles; they will run and not grow weary, they will walk and not be faint."

No matter the challenges you face today, tomorrow will come.

NOTES FROM THE AUTHOR

Over the past few years, I've learned that hard, long and challenging days can, and will end. You have an opportunity to make the next day better by taking what you've learned from the previous one. No matter the situation, have peace in knowing that living to see another day is not guaranteed, but every wake of breathing air is a new opportunity to turn your life into how you desire. Hunt the good stuff by figuring out ways to make sure that the next day doesn't turn into a repetitive situation.

Make it a priority to create a fresh opportunity for yourself. We can't always stop a situation from occurring, but we do have the opportunity to make sure that history does not repeat itself. When times get rough, just remember that the bad news you heard today won't be so bad tomorrow. The harsh words used during anger will not be remembered in its entirety tomorrow. Yesterday's pain won't be today's pain. Take every challenge and every day for what it is. Learn and develop ways to make your life better. We all experience challenges but the way you deal with those challenges will determine your level of peace and happiness.

Make the decision today to say "I will endure whatever it is I must endure but tomorrow, I will make it better than it is right now."

Call to Action

- For this week's challenge, capture moments in the week that may seem like challenges when those challenges are known.
- At the end of the week, write out the outcome and compare them. Did those situations take a hard turn towards the end of the week? Did issues smoothen themselves out?
- Did challenges turn into opportunities? Did issues phase out? Were some of those challenges actual challenges or did they turn out for the best?

WEEK 11
VALIDATING YOUR GROWTH-ISOLATE, REFLECT, AND PUT IN ACTION

Philippians 5:6 "being confident of this that he who began good work in you will carry it on to completion until the day of Christ Jesus."

Growth requires isolation, reflection, and action.

NOTES FROM THE AUTHOR

There will come a time in your life when you will reach a point where your growth is evident to others as well as yourself. You will have that moment when you look up and realize how far you've come, how your past experiences have shaped you, and how you're simply no longer the same.

There will be a time where people will bring your growth to your attention without you having to ask. There will be a time when people are asking you how you made it or asking what brought on your change. Take it all in and remain humble. Take it as validation that God is working on you and using you as his example. Understand that testimonies come in many different shapes and sizes. You don't have to make it on the big screen to be considered a testimony and you don't have to make millions to be considered blessed.

A recovering alcoholic or drug addict is not just testimonies, but they are present-day heroes with an imaginary cape. Recovering addicts provide others with hope. Growth can never be too small. It can be used to impact your community.

Many people remember me as the free-spirited party girl with a huge chain that read my name. With that reputation, came great memories to those in which grew up with me especially my fellow Morganites.

But today, people recognize and respect me as a Captain in the United States Army and often compare and contrast the growth. I thank God for leading me down this path and could not have done it without him. Growth required me to pray, take time to think and make good decisions. I didn't realize the transformation that has been occurring over the years until other people acknowledged my growth. People from college and high school informed me of how much I've changed. I used that as confirmation and continued to allow God to use me as his walking testimony.

I've learned to use feedback from others to give me clues to whether or not I'm on the right path and continued to operate in that space. When you allow God's hand to direct your life, others will be able to see the difference between who you were and who you are today.

Call to Action

- Take this week to reflect on who you were and who you are today.
- Have you allowed God to lead your life?
- What significant changes have you seen in doing so? If you're still

struggling with giving God full control of directing your life, jot down how you're going to allow him to move you in to the right direction. *Be movable.*

WEEK 12
HOW JUDGING A BOOK BY ITS COVER CAN KEEP YOU FROM CONNECTING TO GREATNESS!

Matthew 7:2 "For in the same way judge others, you will be judged, and with the measure you use, it will be measured to you."

Taking the Additional Time to get to know those you encounter during your Journey.

Never judge a person because you never know what a person has been through or the blessing that they may be delivering.

NOTES FROM THE AUTHOR

If you let anyone tell you, all I did at the captain's career course was eat and sleep. What my classmates did not know at the time was that I was in an emotionally and mentally abusive relationship. I barely had the energy to make it to class every day. I spent the majority of my nights wide awake either arguing or being forced to stay up to watch television. Yes, forced to stay up to watch television.

The person that I was in a relationship with at the time would start arguments with me and if I tried to get some sleep, he would argue that I was going to bed way too early and if I passed out, he would make me feel bad for not staying up with him. If it wasn't going back and forth about staying up late, we were probably arguing about some other unnecessary issues. I used to be completely drained every single day. I didn't want to work out during PT and I did not want to sit in class for hours on end. I couldn't gather enough energy to make it through. I fell asleep every day almost every other hour. I was drained. My soul was drained. I lost out on networking opportunities because I was too drained to start or hold conversations during class and I didn't make any plans after class. I also lost out on the opportunity to rank the top 3 in my class which was my original goal.

I was just making it through, praying that I would at least pass the course. I can only imagine how my classmates and instructors viewed my work ethic or the seriousness of my career. This was the first time in my life that I was the person who in my opinion wasn't performing. I knew my situation but no one else did.

For those who know me, they would be shocked to know that I was okay with just receiving mediocre results. In this moment of my life, I was okay with standard results. I passed the career course by prayer alone.

I know for a fact that I should not have made it out, but God spared me the chance because he knew that my mindset and present work ethic was temporary. God knew that I would make it through, and I am so thankful. I now take a second before I place a title on someone. I try to initiate a conversation to gain a better understanding of their current position in life.

For example, there may be some homeless people living on the street that had it all together at some point in their lives. Some of them may have even graduated from college. Life happens, situations happen. Take a moment to get to know people and be hesitant when placing a title until you've come to understand the reason behind who they are.

Call to Action

We are not perfect, and we all go through seasons, don't step on someone while they're down. Find ways to bring them up. Take some time this week to brainstorm your effective approach to developing a way to learn people for their true selves rather than your perceived impressions.

WEEK 13
EMBRACING CHANGE AND MAKING IT WORK FOR YOU

2 Corinthians 5:17 "Therefore, if anyone is in Christ, the new creation has come: The old has gone, the new is here."

The greatest part about change is that you're given a new opportunity each day to try it all over again.

NOTES FROM THE AUTHOR

It's never too late to change. I've found that I've wasted good valuable time in life by shying away from change. I procrastinated because I allowed fear to overpower the results of change. I knew that change required sheer discipline and consistency. Let's be real, lacking both of those characteristics daily has caused me to get into this position in the first place. I scared myself out of change. I was afraid that I would not succeed in my attempt to change. Until one day, I realized that I was limited in my ability to change. *I was the holdup.* If you are anything like me, a perfectionist, you probably battle with yourself often.

I will tell you that you are strong and capable of changing. Don't worry about failing because your attempt to get better is more honorable than to not try at all. Once you truly see and believe that you are in control of your rate of change, you will break through those barriers. Trust in your process and keep the faith. Every successful person has experienced that moment in time where they had to step out on faith and just change. Don't hold off until tomorrow. No process is perfect, stay focused and keep at it. You may not see results immediately. But then again, nothing good comes easy. You will look up one day and appreciate that you started your process to change today rather than tomorrow. If you try and don't succeed, try again.

Call to Action

- Take a moment to jot down areas of your life that require change?
- Do you need better time management?
- Do you need to change eating habits?
- Work out consistently?

WEEK 14
SPEAKING POWER INTO YOUR MIND

Proverbs 15:4 "The soothing tongue is a tree of life, but a perverse tongue crushes the spirit."

Whatever you tell your mind, your body will follow.

NOTES FROM THE AUTHOR

You are as strong as your mind tells you. You can knock down a wall if your mind believes it. I've experienced several situations where I have had to talk myself through it. I've either talked myself into something or I've convinced myself that I couldn't do something. One thing is for sure, whatever I convinced my mind, my body followed. For example, I told myself that I couldn't make it at mile 11 during air assault school because my mind believed that the load that I carried was too heavy. Those words resulted in me failing the course. But when I told myself that I would graduate with my master's degree while going through an emotionally abusive relationship with no energy to think, I mastered it.

When I sit back and think of all of my accomplishments and failures alike, I've realized that my mind played a major role in the outcome. I've started to realize that taking two minutes out of my day to tell myself that "I can do it" changes my entire day. In reverse, waking up with a negative mindset will result in failure too. When you dig deep and understand that your future lies in the words you speak, you will begin to speak positivity and prosperity rather than worry and doubt.

Call to Action

- This week write down your goals for next week.
- Start your day off by telling yourself that you can accomplish all of the goals set out for that particular day. At the end of the week review your list.
- How many goals did you fail to meet?
- I will confidently say fewer than you expected and more than you accomplished last week!
- Let this be a week of productivity.

WEEK 15
TURNING FAILURE INTO MOTIVATION

2 Corinthians 4:9 "We are persecuted, but God does not leave us. We are hurt sometimes, but we are not destroyed."

Failure has an interesting way of creating motivation.

NOTES FROM THE AUTHOR

As I reflect on my success or lack thereof, I've realized that failure played a key role. Whether I woke up one morning with a made-up mind to succeed under any means necessary or I turned my alarm clock off because I needed a few more minutes until I faced reality; both actions were as a result of a failure.

My philosophy: Failure is not an option.

I am not okay with failure; I don't accept and quite honestly, the thought of failure makes me sick. With that in mind, failure has been a primary factor that drove me to accomplish my goals. There have been times in my life where I've failed publicly or behind closed doors. Neither one of those experiences felt better than the other because I look at failure the same.

However, I encourage you to allow failure to work for you.

Use failure to spin your success. When you are publicly embarrassed because you've failed at doing something or failed to measure up to a certain standard in front of others, allow it to fuel your desire to succeed. Think of how good it will feel to show the very ones in which you failed that you are resilient and confident enough to fail and grow from your failure.

A person who can display growth after failure is strong.

It takes courage to continue to push after you've failed; finding a way to accept failure while managing to continue to push forward isn't easy. Just two weeks ago, I submitted an email about the status of my fleet's tires which caused a spotlight thorough inspection of my maintenance program and company.

I received some backlash from my unit in the rear and had to explain myself to a variety of people who outranked me. *I was embarrassed.* I had an entire battalion of key leaders that not only found out about my situation but produced a maintenance news article that used my company as a mockery. It was truly embarrassing; the action was unprofessional, and no one backed me. I reported the article, and nothing was done to the person who wrote the article. That is when I realized- if you don't give the crowd anything to say they can't talk.

Although the condition of my company's tires were not my fault and I attempted to fix the issues before departing, this situation ultimately made me an even more sound leader in my job. I learned.

I further realized how quickly bad news travels- quicker than good news.

I used that embarrassing moment to ensure that they never received another chance to treat me the same way again. I have and will continue to kill them with kindness. I turned public humiliation as a Commander into fuel that I used to ensure that I am always on top of my game. I could have allowed the public embarrassment to make me bitter, but I came to a closure with the understanding that some people enjoy the entertainment of someone else's failure. I've decided to not be the failure that fulfills that desire. As passionate as I am about my job, it did hit me hard when I realized that so many people were waiting to point fingers at me and that I lacked the support of my unit from the rear. Despite my perceived failure, God was there the entire time. I was strong enough to brush off all negativity and keep moving forward.

There are plenty of people who used my situation as the highlight for the week. Some people were too cowardly to accept responsibilities for their part. However, I took all the responsibility, all of the blame, and all of the embarrassment. I stood strong and endured. I learned to never allow failure to burn me out but to fuel me into a greater version of myself. I turned my failure into success.

Call to Action

- Take this week to turn setbacks into wins.
- List challenges that you were able to use as lessons learned or opportunities for growth.

WEEK 16
WALKING IN YOUR BLESSINGS

Isaiah 41:10 "So do not fear, for I am with you; do not be dismayed, for I am your God. I will strengthen you and help you; I will uphold you with my righteous right hand."

Don't be afraid to walk in the blessings that God has finally released unto you.

NOTES FROM THE AUTHOR

There have been times in my life where I spent the majority of my days in tears— tears of hurt, disbelief, regret, unforgiveness of myself and others. I've shed many tears for many reasons. I've also found myself in difficult times where I've found it difficult to live and enjoy blessings that God may have bestowed my way. I remember a time where I felt bad or cautious about being happy because I felt that it was unreal or that I was undeserving. I am here to tell you that it is okay to enjoy your blessings. We need to take daily quiet time to reflect on events or people who are entering and exiting our lives. We need time to compare last year to this year. It is important for quiet time because that is usually the time when you realize that God has blessed you with something you've prayed for and you have every right to rejoice in that blessing. We have to get our minds out of the pattern of giving so much energy to our defeats or our losses. Wins are blessings and blessings are meant to make you feel good. Identify when God is blessing you and don't feel bad for feeling good at the moment.

It is okay to be cautious, but trust that God's word never goes in vain. Even if you receive it when you're not expecting, it doesn't mean that you don't deserve to receive it. Keep your mind and heart open to the thought of accepting blessings. With that mindset, you will be expecting more blessings than defeat which will promote a healthy mind and way of thinking. Sometimes, we kill our chances of enjoying a blessing because we've trained our minds to focus on the negative. We ultimately affect our ability to see when everything is working for our good.

Call to Action

Take this week to live in the moment.

- Focus on the areas in your life that God has blessed you.
- Train yourself to enjoy those blessings.
- Train your mind and speak to your mind in a way that you learn to have joy in a time of prosperity. Remember, we are so quick to give energy to those areas in our life that's caused us challenges, learn to give thanks to the areas that's been going well. We were not put in this world to suffer.

WEEK 17
TRUSTING GOD'S PLAN FOR YOU

Proverbs 3:5 "Trust in the LORD with all thine heart, and lean not unto thine own understanding.

If you knew the plans God had for your life, you would take your hand out of the cookie jar.

NOTES FROM THE AUTHOR

I used to be one of the most impatient people that I knew until I continued to experience the aftermath of impatience. Impatience led me to make bad decisions. I've learned to take a bit more time with making both short- and long-term decisions and not to decide over temporary situations. The problem with impatience is that most decisions are made without knowing or understanding the entire picture.

For good decision making to occur, you have to understand the bigger picture. It is almost impossible for one to understand the bigger picture without being patient. I would like to believe that my lack of success at the US Army's air assault school was due to not allowing the training process to take its course. I rushed the training, giving myself roughly 30 days before the school date. Had I given myself 90 days to allow for late nights at work, time in the field, and some time off to rejuvenate, I am more than certain that I would have been successful.

My body would have had plenty of time to adjust to the weight and I would have been mentally and spiritually ready. The second time that I returned to complete the 12-mile ruck; I failed because I rushed to get to the next opportunity to prove those that saw me fail the first time, wrong. I was so focused on proving that I could pass that I did not spend the time required to prepare for a second shot. My body was already beaten down the first time that I did not allow for much recovery, and I took another physically intense beating to the body.

The second time that I returned to Air Assault School, I completed fewer miles during the 12-mile ruck then I did the first round because I did not allow my body to heal. I was so focused on proving myself that I failed to properly train. I've learned the importance of spending more time on preparation to allow for execution to go smoothly.

The level of energy and the amount of attention that you put into something during the preparation phase determines what you will reap later. Just like everyone else, I become anxious about the outcome, but to guarantee success, you have to learn how to ignore the outcome to allow maximum focus towards the preparation.

Failing to allow the process to take its course can cause the end state to not work on your behalf. Take it from someone who knows, impatience will not contribute to a successful ending. Take your hand off it, prepare for what's in store and trust the process. How many tests have you studied for and failed? The answer is probably none. So, trust that the time you spend to prepare yourself for what's to come will work out on your behalf. What big event do you have coming up next week?

Call to Action

- Take time to prepare and practice patience.
- Following the event, write down the results.
- Was it successful or did it fail?
- Did you take it slow by properly preparing instead of rushing right into it and hoping for the best?
- Think of ways to keep yourself occupied during the wait. Write those ideas down so that you can reflect on them when you need a small reminder.

WEEK 18
CHERISHING ORDAINED CONNECTIONS WITH OTHERS

Ephesians 4:2-3 "Be completely humble and gentle; be patient, bearing with one another in love. Make every effort to keep the unity of the Spirit through the bond of peace."

The world has a funny way of connecting people from all walks of life.

NOTES FROM THE AUTHOR

I think it's safe to say that one of the most memorable experiences of a Soldier is our interaction with people from different walks of life. Thinking back on my career makes me smile, knowing that I've crossed paths with people from different walks of life, cultures, beliefs, and experiences that led them to the same path as myself.

I truly enjoy hearing about other people's life stories or listening to their "why" for serving in the army, re-enlisting or continuing their career in the army. It amazes me that God had a plan for all of our lives and somehow our paths crossed one another. I truly believe that we meet people for a reason and that although all interactions are not meant to be long term~ all interactions serve a purpose. As I sit here and type this very passage, I am in a car with a group of Soldiers from different regions of the United States, different age brackets, and ranks. What amazes me is that we can and have learned from one another.

Although I am the oldest person in the vehicle, I have the least amount of experience with raising a child. Often, I overhear their conversations in regard to how they handle different situations that pertain to making decisions for their child/children. Although they may be young in rank, they too have a lot of knowledge, life and technical experience regarding their job. That in itself amazes me. It amazes me because I truly believe that I would limit my ability to learn or grow if I didn't take time to listen to what they had to say. I would truly be doing myself an injustice if I failed to have conversations with them because of rank or age. In reality, I've learned a lot from my Soldiers. My Soldiers are strong. I have one Soldier who still manages to smile although she has a young daughter that she had to walk away from to perform this deployment. Daily she wakes up and puts her all into this job even when she doesn't feel like it. I sometimes ask myself, "could I be as strong as her?" Or "Could I have decided to walk away?" Because of Soldiers like her, I wake up and choose to put my issues to the side, to be strong and continue to push for those who carry a heavy burden. I try to find ways for our Soldiers to feel good about what they are doing. As a leader, that becomes quite difficult because oftentimes, they are going through situations that are out of anyone's control. I respect them for making those hard decisions and as their leader, I can honestly say that some of those decisions would be hard for me to make. I learn from their bravery, strength, knowledge and skills daily. Due to their sacrifice, I owe it to them to also sacrifice my personal needs and issues. I must remain present, strong, and consistent in my leadership style. I owe it to my Soldiers to carry the load understanding that they are already carrying one daily.

Call to Action

- Take some time this week to write down a few names of people in which you can learn or grow. Think outside the box. You'll be surprised that your day is full of opportunities for growth.

WEEK 19
UNDERSTANDING YOUR PURPOSE

Proverbs 20:5 "The purpose of a person's heart are deep waters, but one who has insight draws them out."

Understanding your purpose will provide guidance even when some days don't seem so clear.

NOTES FROM THE AUTHOR

Have you ever felt like you had a list of goals, but you didn't see much progression in accomplishing those goals? There was a time where I had a list of goals. Eventually, I came to grips that all my goals did not serve a purpose. Some goals looked good on paper but did not directly relate to one another. Having a list of unrelated goals is just as bad as failing to accomplish goals. Attempting to accomplish unrelated goals display horizontal progression and no vertical progression. Horizontal progression is accomplishing goals that keep you on the same level and doesn't contribute much to increasing knowledge, increasing skills, or sharpening gifts and talents. Those who continue to accomplish horizontal goals are those who are okay with not elevating to the next level. Horizontal progressors are those who are probably afraid of stepping outside of the box and after a while, max out on pointless goals that fail to elevate them any higher than their current position in life. Those who progress vertically and align those goals with that mindset are those who break barriers. Vertical progressors are typically people who are not afraid to go against the grain, are willing to take risks, and accomplish goals that are related to one another with an ultimate end state. *Vertical progressors are game-changers.* To change the game, one must have a defined end state and a plan to get there. I've learned to choose goals based on where I planned on going or what I planned to do, rather than what looks good. If the end state doesn't serve a purpose, why should one allocate time or energy to it?

Remember, we all serve a purpose. Once you identify your purpose, you will be able to determine and establish your plan to vertically progress. Let's start your journey by identifying your purpose.

Call to Action

- Write down skills or hobbies that you've noticed your greatest impact on others and what comes easy for you.
- Pray on those areas and ask God to reveal your purpose to you.
- Wait for confirmation!
- What God has purposed for you will not take more than what you will be given to do it!

WEEK 20
LEARNING TO PUSH PASS FEAR

2 Timothy 1:7 "For the Spirit God gave us does not make us timid, but gives us power, love, and self-discipline."

Don't count yourself out before you count yourself in.

NOTES FROM THE AUTHOR

How many opportunities have you given up before trying? How many opportunities did you let slip through your fingers because you did not believe that you could succeed?

At times, your goals may seem scary or too far out of reach. Sometimes, you may miss an opportunity because you scare yourselves out of it. When you are prepared for the challenge then you can take a moment to map out your goals. Please note~ it won't come easy. Nothing comes together all at once (words of my mother.)

Everything comes together well when goals are set, prayers are prayed, and the motivation to succeed is high. You will forever be your biggest supporter. Sometimes you may be the only person that can see your vision. You may be the only person that believes that your prayers, dreams, or aspirations will become a reality. I am here to tell you that your prayer, dream, or aspiration can be your reality. You can make it happen and you are one step closer to your goal! Don't give up!

Call to Action

- Take this week to think of that one goal or aspiration that you have been putting off.
- Develop a plan that includes milestones that will allow you to see your progress.
- You can do it.

WEEK 21
DEVELOPING A WINNER'S MINDSET

Romans 8:28 "And we know that for those who love God all things work together for good, for those who are called according to his purpose."

You'll win some and you'll lose some but it's up to you to feel like a winner regardless.

NOTES FROM THE AUTHOR

I am not the first person to tell you that losing does not feel good. I don't like to lose and I definitely, do not like to lose in a public forum. Losing can make you feel insecure or unfit to perform or fill a position. Losing is always looked at from a negative perspective, but have you thought of going against the grain by taking an experience that resulted in a loss and turning it into a win? Think about it.

Losing takes courage and strength to endure. When you overcome a loss, you've proven yourself to be a winner because not everyone is strong enough to handle it.

I recently just experienced a period of losing as Company Commander. There is nothing more embarrassing than losing in front of your company. The force in which I felt like I was losing was due to deciding to choose my Soldiers' safety over my reputation. I was publicly humiliated, many people spoke negatively behind my back, and many did not stand up to my defense.

But God did.

He kept me strong; he kept me in the fight.

There were moments through my losing period where I felt like giving up.

I felt like I wanted to give my position to someone else because I could not bear the heaviness of disappointment in myself.

I could not begin to understand how I ended up in the situation, but I realized that God will get the glory in the end and all I had to do was stand.

So, I stood and weathered the storm and I was able to write the passage through strength, and not weakness.

There will be moments in life where you feel like you are losing or that you are a loser, but you must remember that to become a winner, you must be strong enough to endure a loss.

Call to Action

- Take this week to think of areas in your life that made you feel like a failure. Think of the wins that came from that situation. Train your mind to have the winner's mindset no matter what. You've overcome those situations and still pushed forward. You won the battle!

- The next time you feel defeated, look over this list.
- How many battles have you one?!

WEEK 22
PROPERLY MEASURING YOUR STRENGTH

Ephesians 6:10 "Finally, be strong in the Lord and his mighty power."

Strength is not found in one's physical capabilities, strength comes from the ability to overcome challenges while remaining hopeful.

NOTES FROM THE AUTHOR

There was a time in my life where I measured my strength based on the pounds that I was able to bench or how fast I was able to run. I used to believe that others measured my strength and recognized me as a strong person by my physical stature and abilities. Through experiences, I've learned that overcoming challenges were the moments that strengthened me. I've learned from late-night tears and failure. In those moments, I chose to continue to push forward with hope and expectations. In those moments, I revealed my strength.

I remember my first major break up.

I returned from deployment and a few months later, a relationship that I fought so hard to get through, ended. There were times where I didn't want to get out of the bed in the morning, let alone go to work. I dreaded taking showers, I didn't want to look for my uniform, and I felt completely alone and broken. I was single, an active duty First Lieutenant living far away from her family in Texas. The only thing that kept me going was my connection with my family and my relationship. A relationship that I believed was going to turn into a beautiful marriage one day, at least that's what I thought. I was so stuck on making it work that I didn't realize how tired and weak I was becoming by holding on to something that was not meant for me.

At that time in my life, I felt weak and defeated. I didn't have anything left but a prayer— a prayer for hope and wisdom to sail through.

I spent many nights in my room in tears, asking God to show me why he kept me isolated. I was angry I felt that everyone one else was getting married and having children. I felt that the women who were around me were blessed; they found Mr. Right and Mr. Right married them. I could not understand why other women would complement everything I had going on, but I had everything but a relationship, let alone a family of my own. Being an active-duty officer made it even more difficult to go through a break up with having to plan and attend family-oriented events in once a month. It always seemed like I was the lucky one to get selected to host the family events for the battalion, yet it was awkward attending them because I didn't have a family yet. During that break-up, I was literally in a twilight zone. I could not understand why it seemed like even people who did not deserve a good person in their life had someone. The very people who were either cheating or just not good people in general- were in relationships. *During that moment of weakness, I learned to not lean on my understanding, I learned the power of prayer.*

I remember the day that I made a declaration. I told myself that on

November 01, 2014 that by the end of that month, I had to come out of bondage. I understood that it would be painful; I understand what I would go through, but I refused to allow this break up to ruin my future. This break up caused me to question myself and other people. I could have been internally damaged for a lifetime if I didn't strengthen myself in prayer and speak life into my soul.

From the day that I promised myself and God that I would push through my current trial no matter the cost, I went from a broken and torn soul to a strong woman of God.

This very situation showed me the power of prayer.

It showed me that a situation that would normally cause some people to contemplate suicide, lose focus, or lose everything that they've worked for, could be solved with prayer and hope!

I spoke life into a situation that didn't have life.

I spoke positivity into a situation that seemed hopeless and unfixable.

I pulled myself out of bed every day.

I prayed morning, night, and mid-day. Every day, I strengthened myself through prayer, positive thoughts, and visions of a hopeful future.

I want you to know that if you can see it, you can have it.

I was able to speak myself out of a broken place and by November 31, 2014, I was completely healed from a break up that I had with someone who I loved and trusted dearly and until this day, I've never looked back. I don't feel the loss. I realized that what seemed like a loss was a gain.

I gained my happiness, my self-worth, and peace of mind.

Call to Action

- Take this week to write a description of your level of strength.
- What keywords or scenarios come to mind when you think of your strength?
- For your areas of weakness, how can you turn them into strengths?

WEEK 23
LEARNING TO IDENTIFY DISTRACTORS THROUGH REFLECTION

1 Corinthians 10:13 "No temptation has overtaken you that is unusual for human beings. But God is faithful, and he will not allow you to be tempted beyond your strength. Instead, along with the temptation, he will also provide a way out, so that you may be able to endure it."

Reflection is required to help you identify the distractors that throw you off your game.

NOTES FROM THE AUTHOR

Have you ever wondered what caused you to end up where you are? Have you ever felt like you were much further behind than where you planned? Are you someone who feels like you are running the same course and ending up in the same direction? Well believe it or not, sometimes life requires you to take a moment to reflect on your past. Think about the moments in life when you saw little progress. Nine times out of ten, the same factor(s) that threw you off your game before are likely to throw you off again if you don't confront it. For me, I noticed that I used to fall off my game over and over again when I was going through either relationship issues or break-ups. During my weakest physical, mental, and spiritual moments, I struggled the most to be my best version. Being with the wrong person would physically drain me due to arguments and disagreements. With a lack of focus~ I also struggled with both business and personal projects.

Lastly, I noticed that the relationships that drained me were with people that I did not seek God's approval.

We were unequally yoked, and it showed!

Being with the wrong person caused a lot of heartache and distractions. Now that I've identified the factor that causes me to fall off my game, I made it a priority to ensure that the people in my life are of good quality and that I pray and ask for God's confirmation.

Call to Action

- What causes you to fall off your game?
- Think of the moments in your life where your progressed ceased. What was the result?
- Do those moments have the same common factor?
- Once you identify what hinders your progression, identify a way to conquer it.

WEEK 24
TAKING "NO" FOR AN ANSWER

2 Timothy 4:7 "I have fought the good fight, I have finished the race, I have kept the faith."

I've never taken "no" for an answer.

NOTES FROM THE AUTHOR

I've never taken "no" for an answer has always been my life's motto and it's gotten me very far. I've never accepted a close door as a reason not to continue to push through. Nor have I ever allowed defeat to keep me down. Sometimes, I forget the level of challenge that I to overcome in order to receive my blessing(s.) When blessings come, many times the pain and the associated struggles disappears too.

As a young girl I would set goals and would not stop until I accomplished them. I was always the one student that applied for the contest or attempted at goals that seemed impossible to others but attainable to me.

In first grade, there was an announcement made regarding a poetry contest held by the Martin Luther King school complex. The contest consisted of developing a poster or poem that was directly correlated with stopping drugs and violence in the neighborhood and streets. The prize included a free limousine ride to the Trump TaJ Mahal in Atlantic City at the time for free dinner and a magic show. The winner would also be given the option to bring one person free of charge. When I heard that announcement, I knew that I had to go after it. The contest specifically stated that there would be one winner per grade. I had it set in my mind that I would be the winner for the first-grade class. At that time there was (from my memory) four other first grade classes with at least 30 people in each class. I did not see competition, I didn't care who was more talented, smarter, or more creative. I had a goal in my mind and that goal was to win. I did not take no for an answer. I didn't let the other kids around me deter me from submitting a product. I went home, wrote a poem about having a drug free school system. I submitted my product on time. The following week they announced the winners on the intercom by grade. When they announced the first-grade winner, the winner was (I remember hearing it clear as day) "Debora Nelson", Ms. Taylor's class. I remember the excitement and joy. I could not wait to rush home to inform my mother that I had won a contest to take her to the magic show and free dinner with me and that we would ride to the Taj Mahal in a limousine.

I can't remember how long after, but I still remember that day. My mom had me in my best gown with my hair done and that day I met Donald Trump (who is now the President of the United States) and rode in the limousine to the Taj Mahal for a free magic show and dinner. It was so worth the experience at the age of seven. I saw the goal; I put my mind on the goal and blocked everyone else from obtaining that goal.

Call to Action

- What "Nos" aren't you going to take this week?
- Start small, build your confidence and create the "I'm not taking no for an answer mentality."

WEEK 25
PERFORMING WHEN CHALLENGED

Luke 21:19 "Stand firm, and you will win life."

"When challenged, perform and do not fold."

NOTES FROM THE AUTHOR

There will be plenty of times in life where you are challenged. Your skill, your abilities, your beauty, and your knowledge will get tried and tested. But it is up to you to not fold. If someone challenges your ability to uphold a certain standard, don't ever step down or count yourself out. Those who show great potential will be challenged often. Want me to let you in on a secret? If someone is challenging you to do something, you can almost guess that they are fully aware of your potential and probably can't believe it for themselves. I've been in a position when someone held my job over my head. Told me that if I did not perform that I would receive a "relieve of the cause." What threw me for a loop was that the conversation started with acknowledging how hard I had worked since being in a new position in a new location. At that moment, I decided to continue to work hard (which is already in my nature) and to never allow "man" to have the power to hold my job over my head. Had I been weak-minded or disconnected from God, I would have lost it especially because of the position that I held at the time.

People can only apply pressure to you or stress you out if you allow them.

Call to Action

Take control of your destiny; take control of your mental, physical, and spiritual health. I've truly learned to focus on pleasing God because people will never be satisfied. Performing when being challenged is not to prove anything but to display what is already in you, which is a winner!

- Take this week to develop your approach to working above standard when tested or challenged.

WEEK 26
SHAPING YOUR TRUE IDENTITY

Proverbs 3: 13 "Happy is anyone who becomes wise- who comes to have understanding."

Allowing people to tell you who you are is like allowing someone to commit identity theft right in front of your very eyes.

NOTES FROM THE AUTHOR

At the age of 30, I am now willing to accept that there are far too many ways in which my identity can be stolen. For many years, I've been led to believe that identity theft was a physical action alone, but life experiences have taught me that identity theft can also be verbalized. Identity theft; essentially is the deliberate use of someone else's identity, with the intent to gain a financial advantage, obtain credit and other benefits in another person's name. Identity theft is generally associated with someone attempting to falsify someone else's identity through the means of documentation.

Let's take it one step further and look at identity theft through the use of words and influence. One may be vulnerable or become a victim of identity theft through the use of words or influence if surrounded by people who do not have good intentions. Ensure that you surround yourself with people who are not attempting to steal the very identity that you've worked so hard to establish. One's identity could be falsified or misrepresented by someone misconstruing someone's character, words, or actions without good intentions. We should find out the reason behind the action of having one's identity stolen or taken without permission. Let's be real, if you have any form of assets or even enjoy your privacy, your number one fear in life is having someone steal your identity. When we think of identity theft, we associate it with a person who has had their source of identity taken without permission. Sources of identification include a social security card, birth certificate, passport, or any sensitive document that is associated with sensitive information.

It is okay if you don't know everything, it is okay if you haven't had the required experience for the assignment in which you were assigned. We can't know every single thing. But there is hope. Sometimes people are driven to elevate their minds to the next level by force. You may find yourself in a position where people may attempt to belittle your existence or paint an inaccurate picture of your level of competency and ability to perform or maybe, even your character. Your reputation is established by the actions of your own as well as the stories told by others who may have interacted with you in the past. It is necessary to truly become aware of your strengths and weakness to refrain from accepting a falsified identity. Falsified identities are created by other people's perceptions or opinions and not necessarily by fact.

Call to Action

This week write down who you know yourself to be.

- Write down your strengths and weaknesses.

- If you have moments or days where you began to question who you are, read the notes that you've taken as a reminder of how great you are and most importantly who you are.

- Believe it or not, life can happen so fast that you may forget. As you grow, revisit this section and make updates.

WEEK 27
FIGHTING A WAR WHILE TIRED

Isaiah 40:29 "He gives strength to the weary and increases the power of the meek."

To win a war, you have to fight even when you're tired.

NOTES FROM THE AUTHOR

Have you ever experienced the feeling of pushing through a challenging situation at minimum strength? In reality, those who win are not at their maximum potential. Those who win wars are those who gave it everything they got until they had no more to give. It takes a strong person to continue to walk up a downward slope. It takes a strong person to close a window in the middle of a hurricane. Those who continue to push when they thought they didn't have any more to give are stronger than those who fight at their maximum potential. Having minimum strength to get through a battle doesn't mean you're the weaker link. You may have been the person who fought the longest and the hardest. You may have been the person who fought more than one battle at once. When trying to determine whether or not you're a strong person don't forget to assess all the factors that came against you. A person who ran one 400m race compared to the guy who ran a 100m dash run competed in the long jump, and high jump during one track meet can't compare energy levels at the finish line. You also can't lose sight of the fact that often; people don't see the battles that you fight. You should care less about how people view you, continue to put in your all and continue to encourage yourself to stay in the fight. People have a funny way of making you feel like you haven't given enough based on a skewed perspective. They've watched you fight one battle; they've seen you in one way and assume that's all you have against you. Learn to fight behind closed doors and become a finished product on the other side. When you master the ability to fight as you've never fought before, share your story on how you managed to make overcoming and becoming victorious over a situation look easy. I recently had a conversation with someone in regard to how my current deployment was going. I shared that my deployment was tiring but that I was appreciative of the experience. I did not go into detail, referencing the unbelievable sequence of events that occurred over the past four months. She mentioned; your pictures look like your deployment is going great but I guess behind the scenes no one knows how much work goes into it. She was right! Just like in life, when you are going through a series of events that require your undivided attention and maximum energy, you don't have the time to report to everyone. You don't have the time to check in or to inform every one of the many battles that you face. What is important is that you get through without losing yourself and hopefully, without losing others. Once you're out of it, you owe it to the people around you that feed off your energy to share your experiences. There is always someone around that can learn from your battle wounds. Be an inspiration and living testimony. Although you have been through the fire, you dodged a few bullets, you took a few lickings, you got up and you continued to push until you could not push any further. That's how you share victories.

Call to Action

What battles are you currently fighting that is tiring you out?

Take some time this week to develop a new battle plan that will assist you in pushing through it. Keep fighting even when you're tired. You can and will win!

WEEK 28
SUCCEEDING WITH FAILURE

Psalms 119:71 "It was good for me to be afflicted so that I could learn your statutes."

Succeeding isn't possible without failure.

NOTES FROM THE AUTHOR

Just remember that every trial and step in your life contributes to your overall life story. After all that I've gone through, I would not shy away from defeat and disappointment because those are the very factors that push me daily. I would never appreciate blessings if I never felt the ground. I would never appreciate a good job opportunity if I never worked for a horrible boss. I would never appreciate hard-working subordinates if I've never experienced those who took me for granted, downplayed my level of knowledge, or worked secretly behind my back against me. All of those factors greatly contributed to where I am today. I've cried tears of defeat and stood proud in victory, but what I've learned is that the safest place is to remain is in humility. Humility keeps you in a position to learn. Continuous learning is required to move forward and is critical to success.

Humility will keep you grounded, and it will keep you in the position to win. Celebrate your failures because, in those failures, you've learned lessons that will last you a lifetime. When you think about the people who are considered "success stories" or the "greatest of all time", they are usually the same people who were once overlooked or considered a failure at some point. The greatest success stories blossomed from failure. People are inspired by those who manage to rise from the grave and recreate life. You are as strong as you tell yourself that you are and yes, it is far from easy but do understand that you will begin to live your truths. What you speak is what you will live. As much as enduring failure sucks (yes, I said it), it produces the very seeds that produce the greatest flowers.

<u>*Call to Action*</u>

- Write down challenges or roadblocks that you may be currently facing.
- Develop a plan to turn that roadblock into an open gate to opportunity.

WEEK 29
GROWING IN AN UNKNOWN ENVIRONMENT.

Luke 20:43 "Till I make thine enemies thy footstool".

The people who contribute to your growth are not always the same people that you chose to connect with.

NOTES FROM THE AUTHOR

The opportunity to grow can sometimes be unpredictable. We often view growth with our ability to network with the right people but in reality, sometimes the people who contribute to your growth are at times the enemy or people who seem to be the enemy. In this case, an enemy would be anyone who doesn't mean well for your growth or prosperity. *Surprisingly, enemies have the best way of bringing out the best in us in the most painful way.*

I can truly attest that some of the best-learned lessons were in result of my interactions with the enemy. Those people were the very ones that pushed me to dig deep, encouraged me to increase my knowledge in various fields or to develop the fight to prove myself to be everything that they thought I wasn't. Enemies have a funny way of bringing out the best in some people.

Call to Action

Allow any enemies that you may have encountered to challenge you to step up your game and be the person you are called to be.

Take this week to think of those who you currently feel do not have your best interest at heart.

- Write down lessons learned from your interaction with those people.
- How has that person or people contributed to a greater you?

WEEK 30
USING KNOWLEDGE AS YOUR POWER

Proverbs 18:15 "The heart of the discerning acquires knowledge, for the ears of the wise seek it out".

Develop yourself into a knowledgeable force to be reckoned with.

NOTES FROM THE AUTHOR

Like my mother has always told me, "Knowledge is Power." You must remain fully engaged in your area of expertise. Your mind is the key to your elevation, you must expand and expound your thought process during any given time and the only way to do so is to read and seek that information on your own. You will find that your level of knowledge can become an asset because it will enable you to expose other people to opportunities for growth. People tend to cling on and travel with those in which they feel challenged by and those in which they feel are hydrating their droughts; supply water to others.

Congratulations! You are at the end of your 30-week transformation. Look back to where you spiritually, mentally, and emotionally were thirty weeks ago, compared to now. Your knowledge has increased in so many areas! I am beyond proud of you! You took the commitment to change and you did it.

Call to Action

- Use the final pages to compare and contrasts where you are and where you were spiritually, mentally, and emotionally.
- Jot down detailed changes that you've implemented on your journey.
- In what way have you become more knowledgeable?
- In what way have you developed yourself to become a force to be reckoned with?

www.ingramcontent.com/pod-product-compliance
Lightning Source LLC
Chambersburg PA
CBHW022107160426
43198CB00008B/387